LIFE WITH REIKI

THE COSMOS'S SIGNATURE

SURESH SHAIVA

Made with ♥ on the Notion Press Platform
www.notionpress.com

This book is dedicated to all Reiki practitioners and seekers who are on a journey to heal themselves and others. Your commitment to personal growth and well-being inspires me to continue sharing the teachings of Reiki.

To my Reiki teacher, who introduced me to this powerful healing modality and taught me the ways to harness its energy, thank you for guiding me on this path. Your wisdom and support have been invaluable in my Reiki journey.

To my family and friends, who have supported me throughout my journey, thank you for your love and encouragement.

Also this book is dedicated to lord buddha and Dr. Usui

Dr. Mikao Usui - Lord Buddha

Contents

Contents

Foreword

It is with great excitement and a deep sense of purpose that I present to you this book on Reiki. Reiki is an ancient practice that has been passed down from generation to generation for over 2,500 years. It is a gentle yet powerful form of energy healing that has been proven to help alleviate physical, emotional, and mental stress and promote balance and wellbeing.

As you read through these pages, you will learn about the history and philosophy of Reiki, as well as the fundamental principles and techniques that are used in this healing practice. You will also discover how Reiki can be integrated into your daily life to help you manage stress, improve your health and wellbeing, and deepen your spiritual connection.

So, sit back, relax, and allow yourself to be guided on this journey of discovery and healing.

With gratitude and love,

Suresh Shaiva

Preface

Welcome to the world of Reiki, a powerful and transformative practice that has the ability to bring balance and healing to all aspects of our lives. Reiki has its roots in ancient Japan and has been passed down through generations, offering a path to physical, emotional, and spiritual wellbeing.

This book is a culmination of my own personal journey with Reiki and the lessons I have learned along the way. I am honored to share with you the wisdom and knowledge I have gained, and my hope is that it will serve as a valuable resource on your own Reiki journey.

As you delve into the pages of this book, you will discover the history and philosophy of Reiki, as well as the techniques and principles that are used in this healing practice. You will also learn how to integrate Reiki into your daily life, and how it can be used to manage stress, improve your health, and deepen your spiritual connection.

So, whether you are a beginner or an experienced practitioner, I invite you to join me on this journey of discovery and healing. May the wisdom and guidance contained within these pages bring you comfort, peace, and a deeper understanding of the power of Reiki.

With love and gratitude,

Acknowledgements

Before you dive into the content of this book, I would like to take a moment to express my deep gratitude to the many people who have contributed to its creation.

First and foremost, I would like to thank the Reiki Masters who have shared their knowledge and expertise with me over the years. Their guidance and support have been invaluable in helping me to deepen my understanding of this wonderful practice.

Finally, I would like to express my gratitude to you, the reader, for taking the time to engage with this book. It is my sincere hope that it will bring you comfort, healing, and inspiration as you embark on your own Reiki journey.

With gratitude and love,

Suresh Shaiva

Prologue

Reiki, an ancient practice originating from Japan, has the power to bring balance and healing to all aspects of our lives. It is a simple yet powerful form of energy healing that can be used to promote physical, emotional, and spiritual wellbeing.

"Reiki has a rich history that begins with the birth of its founder, Sri Dr. Usui, on August 15, 1865. In 1888, he had a spiritual awakening at Kuruma-maya Hill and started teaching the Reiki system. In 1902, he established the Reiki Healing Center, and in 1922 founded the "Ryoho Gaikkai" Sangha. Sri Usui simplified the Reiki system in 1924, but passed away on March 9, 1926. Meanwhile, Mr. Chuichiro Hayashi was born in 1879, and taught Reiki to Mrs. Havayo Takata in 1936, who went on to teach the Reiki method to 22 students."

CHAPTER ONE

Reiki Origins and Historical Background

Since you bought this book you will have FREE 1-2-1 session for 30 mins with us. (depends available of the slot)

Savikalpa Holistic Center Mysore

Mobile 6364795551/9538735551
Youtube- @ Savikalpaholisticcenter
Facebook Savikalpaholisticcenter

Reiki Origins and Historical Background

[As reported by Hayashi]

The main position of Reiki It was a touch healing method used in India. This is mentioned in many Vedas.

BC In 500 AD Sri Gautama Buddha was healing the suffering through touch healing. This healing system reached Tibet. From there it reached the non-existent continent called Atlanta. After this continent was destroyed by natural disasters, this treatment was not available to the next generation. This kind of touch healing method that continued from here was followed by Jesus Christ, saints and saints, but due to some reasons, this method remained hidden. However, it is good to know that this power originates from India. In the 18th century, in a town called Kyoto in Japan, Dr There was Mikao Usui who was a follower of Gautama Buddha. He used to teach about Christianity to the students in a school belonging to the Christian community.

Then a student asked a question about the Bible. In the Bible, Jesus said that anyone can do the miracles he created, are you doing those miracles? Do you believe it? Dr.|| Usui says he doesn't know about this. This one question begins to haunt Usui. After that he resigned from his job and began to study Christianity in depth. He discusses with the scholars related to that religion, and learns about the great miracles of the Buddha as told in his own religion, Buddhism. For other research, China, Tibet, India come here and discuss with scholars. The palm fronds are examined and studied. Even after studying its secret symbols, he never got complete information about this science.

After devoting several years to his quest for spiritual enlightenment, Dr. Mikao Usui learned about the Jain saints and their teachings. They advised him to meditate continuously for 21 days to attain spiritual siddhi. With a strong determination, Dr. Usui went to the mountain of Kuruma-maya (Kurimai) and began his 21-day meditation journey with 21 small stones as a reminder of each day. He immersed himself in meditation, connecting with spiritual figures like Jesus Christ and Buddha, hoping that the healing he would learn would also work for others.

However, after 20 days of meditation, Dr. Usui was yet to experience any feelings or effects. He was about to give up when suddenly, a bright star appeared in the sky and descended towards him. Dr. Usui ran towards the light, thinking it might be the reward he had been seeking, and stopped there, waiting to see what would happen next.

The light penetrated through Dr. Usui's Sahasrara Chakra and he entered a state of samadhi for a brief moment. The light appeared as a sphere within a circle and Dr. Usui began to experience various sensations and see special symbols. This experience changed Dr. Usui's life and marked the beginning of his journey as the founder of Reiki healing.

After his enlightening experience on Kuruma-maya mountain, Dr. Usui conversed with the radiant light and gained understanding of its purpose and uses. The light told him that the knowledge he had gained should be passed down to future generations, so he went to share his newfound happiness with the Zen saints.

As he descended the mountain, Dr. Usui was hit by a stone, but when he placed his hand on the injured area, the bleeding stopped and the pain subsided, marking his first miracle. Despite not having consumed food and water for 21 days, he was able to eat and drink normally at a hotel, with no negative impact on his health, resulting in his second miracle. The third came when he was able to heal the toothache of the hotel owner's daughter simply by placing his hand on her cheek, which reduced her swelling and relieved her pain.

From this experience, Dr. Usui realized that simply treating people's physical symptoms would not necessarily bring about a change in their behavior or mindset. He realized that in order for true healing to occur, the recipient must also be willing to take responsibility for their own lives and make positive changes.

This realization led Dr. Usui to develop the principles of Reiki, which emphasize the importance of taking responsibility for one's own life and making positive changes. Reiki practitioners are encouraged to work on their own personal growth and development, as well as to offer Reiki treatments to others. This creates a reciprocal relationship where both the practitioner and recipient benefit from the exchange of energy.

The concept of "energy exchange" is an important part of Reiki practice, as it helps to maintain balance and respect in the relationship between the practitioner and recipient. By exchanging energy in some form, the recipient shows their gratitude for the Reiki treatment and helps to maintain the flow of energy in the universe.

Overall, Dr. Usui's experience with the beggars taught him that true healing goes beyond just treating physical symptoms and requires a change in behavior and mindset. This understanding forms the foundation of Reiki practice, and has helped to make it a popular form of energy healing around the world.

This experience taught Usui the importance of valuing the energy that he was giving. By not receiving any form of compensation in return for his healings, the beggars did not see the value in what they had received and did not feel motivated to make any changes in their lives. From this experience, Usui realized that Reiki energy should not be given for free and that there should be an energy exchange. This energy exchange can come in many forms, including monetary compensation, but the most important aspect is that the recipient acknowledges the value of the energy they have received and is motivated to make positive changes in their life as a result.

It is important to note that the idea of charging for Reiki treatment or classes is not universally accepted in the Reiki community. However charging for Reiki is a way to make the practice more accessible and to support the practitioner's livelihood. Ultimately, the decision of whether to charge for Reiki is a personal one, and Reiki practitioners are free to choose what feels right for them based on their beliefs, values, and circumstances. But we recommend to charge as an energy exchnage otherwise, it will not make person to be serious in his path, and it withholds his progression.

CHAPTER TWO

What is "Reiki"

"Ya Devi Sarva Bhuteshu Matru Rupena Samsthita". It is said that there is a power in all living things of this entire earth, which is also agreed by science.

Atoms are made up of particles consisting of protons, neutrons, and electrons, which give the atom energy.

That means there is energy in every particle. We can call this Reiki energy as Cosmic energy, healing energy, prana sakti, divine energy, this is a wonderful energy that controls the whole world.

The origin of Reiki is believed to be from India, even though it is a Japanese science. The word "Reiki" is derived from two Japanese words: "Rei," meaning universe or world, and "Ki," meaning energy or power. This energy is present in everyone from birth, but due to various reasons, it can become blocked and cause physical and mental problems. Reiki initiation involves cleansing a person's energy field and restoring the flow of energy, enabling the person to become a Reiki channel. This can lead to improvements in health, mental condition, finances, relationships, and help eliminate negative habits.

CHAPTER THREE

The Five Principles of Reiki

Just for today, I will not be angry.

Just for today, I will not worry.

Just for today, I will be grateful.

Just for today, I will do my work honestly.

Just for today, I will be kind to every living thing.

These principles are considered guidelines for living a fulfilling and harmonious life and are often repeated in Reiki practice to help focus the mind and promote inner peace.

CHAPTER FOUR

What is initiation?

Reiki initiation is a process that involves a Reiki Master or teacher opening up the student's energy channels to allow the Reiki energy to flow freely. This involves clearing any blockages in the student's energy field and aligning their energy with the universe. After the initiation, the student becomes a Reiki channel and can use Reiki to heal themselves and others. During the initiation, the Reiki Master may use symbols and techniques to facilitate the flow of energy and activate the student's energy centers (chakras). It is important to note that Reiki initiation is a crucial step in becoming a Reiki practitioner and is necessary for the Reiki energy to work effectively.

There are degrees of types in Reiki according to the intensity of the Reiki flow. Reiki – 1 Reiki – 2 Reiki - 3 (3A) Reiki - 4 (3b) Master Training.

Reiki Level 1

In this stage, you will learn various hand positions to perform Reiki treatments on yourself or others. You are required to visit 24 centers for personal Reiki treatments.

Reiki Level 2

In addition to the techniques learned in Reiki Level 1, three Japanese Kanji symbols will be taught. These symbols are considered secret and should not be discussed or mentioned to others. This level is considered to be four to five times more effective than Reiki Level 1, and it grants the student psychic power and the ability to quickly cure diseases.

Reiki Level 3A

This level is even more effective than Reiki Level 1 and 2, and it reveals a powerful fourth secret symbol that can help cure chronic diseases. It also teaches the student the goal of life and techniques for overcoming past life karma.

Reiki Level 3B (or Reiki Level 4)

At this stage, students receive a powerful initiation and learn how to teach Reiki to others. They are also taught a healing initiation technique. Some Reiki masters may refer to this level as 3B. In the past, a 21-day waiting period was required after Reiki attunement, followed by two additional attunements. However, due to the increase in energy on the earth and in humans, some Reiki Gurus now combine Reiki Level 1 and 2 into one course. A 21-day deadline for initiation is still required.

Post initiation

A Reiki practitioner can experience significant changes in their daily life. Physically, mentally, and in their dreams, the practitioner may observe differences. Keeping a diary and self-reviewing every 10 days can help the practitioner recognize these changes and their personal growth.

CHAPTER FIVE

Some Factors To Consider

It is important to note that while giving up certain habits like smoking, alcohol, and meat consumption is not necessary in Reiki practice, it is believed that doing so can enhance the effects of the practice. This is because the idea is to maintain a pure and healthy body, and having these habits may distract from that goal. However, as a person continues to practice Reiki regularly, it is believed that negative habits will naturally fade away. Once a person has been initiated into Reiki, they are considered a Reiki channel for life, and if they stop practicing for any reason, they can resume at any time and continue to offer Reiki treatments to others.

Guidelines for offering medical attention and necessary steps to assist others.

- Wash your hands before and after conducting a Reiki healing session.
- Before the session, communicate with the person receiving the healing and find out what they need.
- Explain the process of Reiki healing to them.
- It is recommended for the person receiving healing to close their eyes and mentally communicate with their soul, allowing Reiki energy to flow.
- Listening to music is optional.

- Begin the session with a prayer and use the Reiki symbols as taught by your Reiki master to finish.
- It's common for the person receiving Reiki to feel drowsy, so allow them to sleep and wake them up gently when the session is over.
- Drink water before and after the session and offer it to the person receiving Reiki.
- Reiki can strengthen relationships and bring financial empowerment, while improving memory and self-confidence.
- Reiki can be performed at a distance using a technique called distance healing.
- Remember, you are not the one who performs the healing, but rather a channel for the Reiki energy to flow through.
- Only offer Reiki to those who request it, and don't perform it for free (except for children, relatives, accident victims, or plants).
- Reiki should be performed in a sacred space, using sandalwood incense and maintaining a calm demeanor.
- Reiki can be performed without any restrictions based on caste, creed, religion, or any other factor.
- It is recommended to keep a distance of three inches, especially when performing Reiki for girls or women

This is why Reiki is so popular

- Reiki boosts immunity and supports physical, mental, emotional, and spiritual wellness.
- Many medically incurable diseases have been reported to be cured through Reiki.
- Reiki is a safe and effective treatment with no adverse side effects.
- During Reiki, the practitioner's illness does not transfer to the patient and vice versa.

- Reiki is not affiliated with any particular religion and has no age restrictions.
- It can be used for self-healing and treating others, as well as for fulfilling personal desires.
- No specific education is required to learn Reiki, but some level of intelligence is necessary.
- Reiki can be applied to various aspects of life, including animals, birds, land, vehicles, homes, businesses, careers, and more.
- Reiki can be performed while performing other activities, such as eating or watching TV.
- Reiki reduces stress and promotes calmness.
- Once initiated, the Reiki energy continues to flow in the person until death.
- Reiki energy cannot be misused and any incorrect use of it will have no effect.
- Reiki can be combined with other modalities, such as meditation, healing, and self-discovery.
- Reiki will flow to where it is needed in the body even if the practitioner does not know where to place their hands. Reiki is a self-luminous energy that is guided by awareness.

CHAPTER SIX

To begin a Reiki practice:

Beofore Healing

- Find a quiet, comfortable space where you can sit or lie down undisturbed.
- Close your eyes and take a few deep breaths, allowing your body and mind to relax.
- Bring your hands into a salutation position, also known as Gassho, in front of your heart.
- Focus on your breathing and allow any thoughts or distractions to pass by without engaging with them.
- Chant the name of your family deity, if you have one, or simply bring to mind a feeling of love and compassion.
- Visualize the Reiki energy flowing from the universe, through your crown chakra, down through your body and into your hands.
- Remember the founders of Reiki, Dr. Mikao Usui, Dr. Chujiro Hayashi, and Hawayo Takata, and honor their teachings.
- Think of your Reiki teacher or Guru and the guidance they have given you.
- Focus on your soul and the soul of others, and send feelings of love and compassion to all beings.
- If you have been taught specific symbols or mantras, use them now to enhance the flow of Reiki energy.

Post Healing

- Thank the Reiki energy for flowing through you and healing the recipient.
- Visualize the Reiki energy sealing the recipient's aura and protection.
- Allow the recipient to rest for a few moments and then gently wake them up.
- Offer them a glass of water to drink.
- Clean the room or area where the healing took place.
- Take a few moments to ground and center yourself.
- Express gratitude for the opportunity to serve and to be a channel for the Reiki energy.
- Remember that as a Reiki practitioner, you are simply a conduit for the energy and that it is the Reiki energy itself that does the healing, not you.

How long should Reiki take?

Reiki has no set duration as it involves the flow of divine energy, which is dependent on the student's level of awareness and mental state. The flow and stopping of energy in the hands can serve as a guide for determining the length of the session. In general, a Reiki session can last anywhere from 3 to 20 minutes, or even longer if the energy flow continues. This may indicate that the area being treated requires more energy or that the issue has become more pronounced. Reiki energy is a remarkable and self-directing force that can find and resolve issues even if the person performing the Reiki treatment is unaware of the specific problem. Simply by placing their hands on the affected area, the energy will flow to where it is needed and resolve the issue.

CHAPTER SEVEN

24 centers of the body

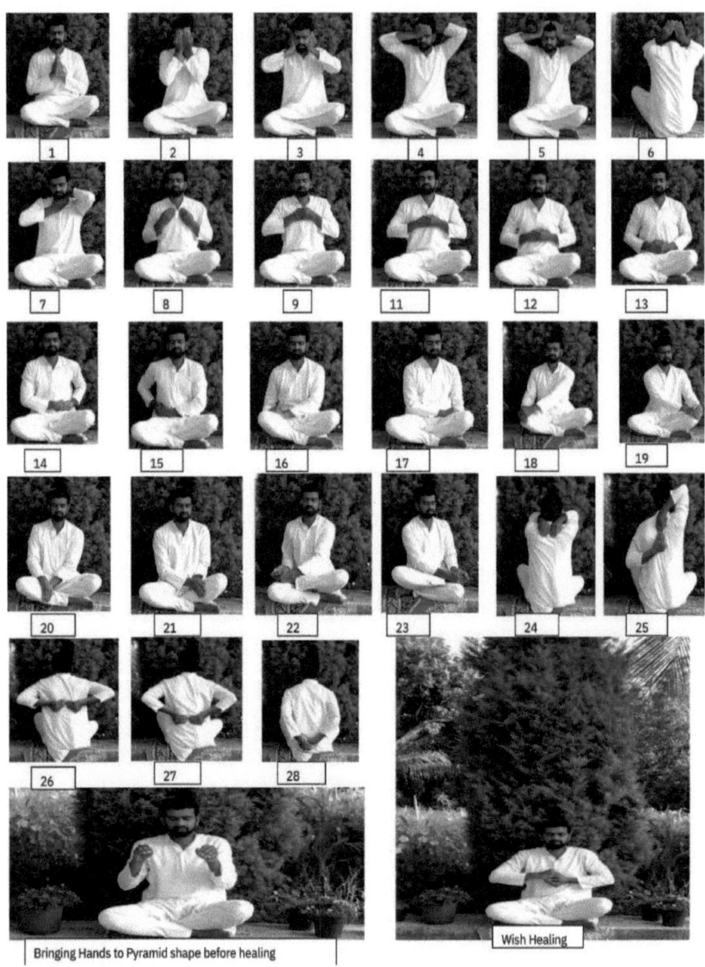

Thank you Kumar- Madikeri

CHAPTER EIGHT

Conclusion

To follow the gratitude steps, one should allow the energy to flow throughout the body while maintaining a smiling demeanor from beginning

Important Notice:

This book provides information on all the methods of receiving and giving Reiki, but merely reading or viewing the book will not enable one to practice Reiki. Reiki can only be practiced after receiving initiation from a qualified Reiki master. Attempting to practice Reiki based solely on the information in a book is unrealistic and ineffective. The information in this book is based on the experiences and observations of many individuals, but if the methods described are not followed correctly, the results may be limited or negligible. It is important to note that even if the methods are followed improperly, there will not be any harmful consequences.

This book serves only as a guide, and the Reiki treatment should be administered based on the specific needs of the recipient. It is important that no medicines should be discontinued without the advice of a medical doctor. Reiki is a non-medicinal form of treatment and should not be used as a substitute for prescribed medicine. However, it can be used as a complementary treatment, and it has been reported that certain medical conditions can be improved through Reiki healing.

Savikalpa Holistic Center Mysore

Mobile 6364795551/9538735551
Youtube- @ Savikalpaholisticcenter
Facebook Savikalpaholisticcenter

CHAPTER NINE

Reiki 2

In Reiki 1, a lot of knowledge is already gained, and Reiki 2 is a crucial next step in the initiation process. This level teaches three Japanese secret symbols, each with its own unique meaning. These symbols are considered powerful and should not be shared with others after they have been learned. They are used to enhance the flow of energy and resolve issues within the recipient's energy centers. These symbols should be treated with reverence and maintained as sacred knowledge.

It is important to note that the symbols themselves do not have any power, and their effectiveness is only achieved through initiation from a certified Reiki master. If the symbols are written down for practice purposes, the sheet should be burned after the session and the ashes should be disposed of by mixing them in water and placing them in a sacred plant. During a treatment, the symbols should be drawn in front of the affected area using one hand (specifically the middle part of the hand, known as the ("Hasta Chakra") while mentally repeating the symbol three times.

Symbol:-1 Chokure

It is called "power symbol". This is the first sign of Usui Reiki, which flows into the root chakra and the physical subtle body of the subtle body.

This symbol is used to strengthen any intention wish. This symbol can be used to protect any place, room, person or valuables from evil spirits.

Symbol:-2 Seheki

This is the 2nd sign of Sri Usui and flows into the Swadhishthana Chakra and into the emotional subtle body. It harmonizes the left and right brain. It relieves you from emotional problems.

Symbol 3: Han Shah Jeshonen

This is the third symbol in the Usui Reiki system and is used to flow energy into the manipuraka chakra and the mental aspect of the subtle body. It has the ability to transcend distance and time, making it useful for providing healing to those at a distance.

To maintain the sanctity of the symbols. It has been given at the last page.

CHAPTER TEN

Various techniques

Energy Balancing

- Touch Healing
- Aura Healing
- Distance Healing
- Group Healing

Energy Balancing

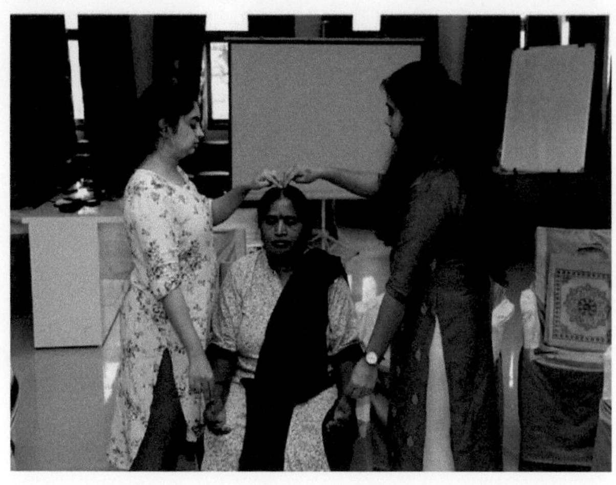

Energy Balancing- Source Our classes

Touch Healing

In Reiki, the practitioner places their hands on their own or another person's body, and recites their names while using the Reiki 1, 2, and 3 symbols. There are 24 positions on the body that can be treated by placing hands on them, starting with a prayer. The practitioner should visualize writing the person's name on their palms and recite it three times while channeling Reiki energy into the area. This should be continued for 2-3 minutes for each part, or until the energy flow stops. The order of these positions can be changed as desired. After treating the 24 positions, the practitioner should guide themselves through self-healing, starting from the top of the body and working their way down. They should then affirm the effectiveness of the treatment and give gratitude before ending the session.

Touch Healing- Source Canva

Aura Healing (Untouch healing)

In this technique, the practitioner uses their hands to treat the aura or the subtle body zone. The Reiki energy flows into this area, and it can be used to treat infections, wounds, burns, and other conditions. When treating female patients, this technique can be used in different orders, such as 1, 2, 3 or 3, 1, 2, 3.

Distance Healing

This technique is useful when treating someone who is far away. The sequence 3-1-2-3 should be used in this case. The person receiving the treatment should sit comfortably and place their hand on the affected area. This method is able to reach the person without being limited by distance or time.

Distnace Healing- Source Canva

Group Healing

When 2 or more people perform the healing at the same time..

Group Healing- Source Our classes

This healing is very helpful for fulfilling a very difficult problem or great desires

- As the person in need of healing is laid down and the linear conductors sit around and give energy, the person will heal quickly.
- A person can be treated in a chain, one behind the other

CHAPTER ELEVEN

Distance Healing techniques

Representation method:

Knowing that the Reiki carrier is that person, Reiki energy can be directed to the place where Reiki is needed as 3, 1, 2, 3.

Sheet method :

Write the person's name, address, address and keep that sheet in the middle of the hand and use 3,1,2,3 for 10-20 minutes of energy.

Hand Method:

The Reiki carrier should imagine the problem of the person in the middle of his hands and give energy like 3,1,2,3 for 10-20 minutes.

Imitations Method :

Keep a copy of the person's portrait / nail / hair, handwriting between the hands and give energy for 10-20 minutes using 3,1,2,3.

Doll Method:

Take a doll of 2-3 feet and give energy for 10-20 minutes using 3,1,2,3 knowing that it is a person who needs the same treatment.

Important

important to note that the sequence of symbols used in touch healing and distance healing are different. In touch healing, the Reiki practitioner should use symbols 1, 2, and 3, while in distance healing, the symbols used should be in the sequence of 3, 1, 2, and 3. There is no strict rule for the length of each session, but it is recommended to spend at least 3 to 20 minutes in each session.

Remember

The Reiki energy does the healing, you are just a conduit for the energy.

It is important to remember that Reiki is not just about healing physical ailments, it also helps to heal emotional and mental pain. So, always approach a Reiki session with a positive and open mind and heart, and let the energy flow where it needs to go. Remember to trust the process and allow the Reiki energy to do its work, without forcing or manipulating the outcome. Finally, always be grateful for the opportunity to heal and help others, and never take the credit for the healing, as it is the Reiki energy that truly does the work.

Having gratitude for what you have is important and it is also good to share some of your wealth with those in need. Contributing a minimum of 1% to a maximum of 10% of your income to those who are less fortunate can bring happiness and positivity in your life. Instead of relying on others to bring you happiness, find joy in making others happy.

CHAPTER TWELVE

Application of Reiki

- For medicines
- to home office
- For children's education
- to a group of people
- Reiki for travel tours
- To build a new house
- Reiki can be done for working / office
- Reiki for business development
- Reiki for childless people
- Don't buy a new car Reiki
- Reiki for Wish Fulfillment / Reiki for Fulfillment of Desires
- Reiki for Marriage Yoga seekers
- Reiki for plants/seeds
- Reiki for pets
- Reiki for students
- Reiki to Earth
- Reiki for Planetary Doshas
- Reiki for edibles
- Reiki for kitchen/cylinders
- Reiki for pregnant women
- Reiki to remove Vastu Dosha
- Reiki for interview / Reiki for placement in current job
- Reiki for debt recovery
- Reiki for relationship improvement

- Reiki for court cases
- Reiki for past lives
- Reiki for the deceased
- Reiki for warding off evils
- Reiki for weight gain / Reiki for weight loss
- Reiki for Chakras
- Reiki for those in ICU
- Reiki for Gurus
- Reiki for the Goddesses

When all other sources of support have failed, where can a person find solace? Reiki provides a helpful answer to this question, as it has the ability to positively impact both the physical and spiritual aspects of a person's life.

Reiki is just one of many Reiki systems that exist in the world, including Karuna Reiki, Usui Reiki, Rainbow Reiki, Moloch's Reiki, Kundalini Reiki, and Chende Reiki. It's important to note that Reiki energy is not freely given or received, but rather must be properly channeled through trained practitioners.

When seeking or providing Reiki, the giver and receiver can opt to chant mantras if they so choose, but it is not a requirement. Reiki is a gentle and divine energy that functions on its own as a natural force, regardless of one's belief in it. However, the practice is enhanced by qualities such as gratitude, trust, and humanity, as it is a form of pure divine love that can only be used for the benefit of others and cannot be misused. Adherence to the five principles of Reiki is crucial for both givers and receivers. It is important to note that practical experience is more valuable than knowledge gained from reading and listening, as the saying goes, "A little practice is better than a lot of knowledge." This means that even a small amount of practice is more beneficial than having a vast amount of knowledge but no hands-on experience.

General Understanding

Reiki energy operates gently on the mind and body, enhancing its overall well-being. While it can be used alongside conventional treatments, it is important to note that it should not replace prescribed medication from a doctor. In some cases, the practitioner may experience a reduction in the need for medication due to the positive effects of Reiki. However, it is essential to follow the advice of a medical professional and not abandon prescribed medications without their approval.

Salt water bath

A salt water bath is a simple yet effective way to purify the mind and body. Simply adding a handful of rock salt to a bucket of water and pouring it over your head can help release negative energy and promote a sense of relaxation and wellbeing. Some people believe that touching the head with salt can cause the hair to turn white, but this is not supported by scientific evidence. Those who bathe in the sea do not experience the same effect as the salt in the sea is dispersed and diluted, making it easier to rinse off. If pouring salt water directly on the head is not feasible, simply taking a bath in the salted water can have a similar impact. Remember to focus your thoughts on releasing negativity while taking the bath.

Selection of Reiki Teacher

It is important to choose a Reiki Guru who is knowledgeable and experienced in their practice. It is also important to consider their ethical standards, their approach to teaching and their overall demeanor. Before choosing a Reiki Guru, it is recommended to do research and take the time to meet with the person to get a sense of their energy and whether they are the right fit for you. A Reiki Guru who comes from Usui's heritage can be an asset, but it is not the only factor to consider. It is important to choose a Reiki Guru who you feel comfortable with and trust.

CHAPTER THIRTEEN

Chakras

Knowing about the subtle body and chakras is crucial for anyone who practices Reiki. To ensure optimal functioning of our physical body, it is important to keep our subtle body in good health. Just like a lamp needs a surrounding light to make its flame visible, our aura, or subtle body, exists around us and contributes to our overall well-being. The aura can also be referred to as haura or outer body.

The seven chakras are energy centers in the human body that are said to control various aspects of physical, emotional, and spiritual well-being. Here is a brief overview of each chakra and its associated properties:

It is important to note that while each chakra is associated with specific physical, emotional, and spiritual functions, they all work together to maintain overall balance and well-being in the body.

Savikalpa Holistic Center Mysore

Mobile 6364795551/9538735551

Youtube- @ Savikalpaholisticcenter

Facebook Savikalpaholisticcenter

Root Chakra (Muladhara):

This chakra is located at the base of the spine and is associated with the color red. It is associated with stability, security, and grounding. It governs basic survival instincts and connects us to our physical bodies and the earth.

Root Chakra (Muladhara):

Sacral Chakra (Svadhishthana):

This chakra is located just below the navel and is associated with the color orange. It is related to our emotional and sexual desires, creativity, and relationships.

Sacral Chakra (Svadhishthana):

Solar Plexus Chakra (Manipura)

This chakra is located in the solar plexus area and is associated with the color yellow. It governs our self-esteem, personal power, and confidence. It also helps regulate our metabolism and digestion.

Solar Plexus Chakra (Manipura)

Heart Chakra (Anahata):

This chakra is located in the center of the chest and is associated with the color green. It is related to love, compassion, and the ability to connect with others. It also governs our physical heart and respiratory system.

Heart Chakra (Anahata):

Throat Chakra (Vishuddha):

This chakra is located in the throat area and is associated with the color blue. It governs communication, self-expression, and the ability to speak your truth.

Throat Chakra (Vishuddha):

Third Eye Chakra (Ajna):

This chakra is located between the eyebrows and is associated with the color indigo. It governs intuition, imagination, and perception. It also helps regulate our sleep patterns and hormones.

Third Eye Chakra (Ajna):

Crown Chakra (Sahasrara):

This chakra is located at the top of the head and is associated with the color violet. It governs spiritual awareness and our connection to the divine. It also helps regulate our central nervous system.

Crown Chakra (Sahasrara):

CHAPTER FOURTEEN

Reiki 3

Reiki 3 builds upon the knowledge and experience gained from Reiki 1 and 2. In Reiki 3, the practitioner has a strong understanding of the first two levels and has already experienced the benefits of Reiki healing. They have learned and are well-versed in the workings of the three symbols introduced in Reiki 2. These symbols are:

Chokure - The Power Symbol, associated with the Muladhara (root) chakra.

Seheki - The Mental Symbol, associated with the Svadhishthana (sacral) chakra.

Han-sha-je-sho-nen - The Symbol of Distance, used for distant healing.

In Reiki 3A, also known as Advanced Reiki Training (ART) or Reiki 3, the practitioner will learn a fourth symbol that has the power to double the power of all the symbols learned in the previous levels. This symbol will provide an added level of potency and effectiveness in healing chronic problems.

During this class, the practitioner will receive a gurudiksha, which is a special initiation ceremony. They will also gain deeper understanding of the background of human problems, allowing them to address root causes and achieve more effective and long-lasting results. The Reiki 3A level is an advanced step for Reiki practitioners and further expands their knowledge and abilities in this healing practic

Usui -the master symbol

The fourth and final symbol in this level of Reiki is known to have powerful healing properties and can greatly enhance the effectiveness of all other symbols. Its purpose is to increase the flow of cosmic energy into the Reiki channel and bring permanent solutions to both the practitioner's and the patient's problems.

The name of this symbol, "always be with me, have mercy on me," reflects its intention to bring comfort and support to those in need of healing. The use of this symbol helps to increase the influence of energy and promote a more powerful and effective flow of Reiki energy.

It is considered a master symbol, and it is recommended to use it before all other symbols for maximum effectiveness. This symbol has the ability to enhance the power of other symbols, making them work more efficiently and effectively.

In addition to its healing benefits, using this symbol can also lead to the development of special healing powers and greater empathy. Reiki practitioners who have learned this symbol have reported experiencing profound and life-changing results in their healing practice.

From this point forward, it is recommended to always use symbol 4 before symbols 1, 2, and 3, whether during a distance healing session or a touch healing session. The order should be 4, 1, 2, 3: 4 being the Reiki Master Symbol, 1 being the Chokure symbol, 2 being the Seheki symbol, and 3 being the Han Sha Je Sho Nen symbol.

It is important to maintain a good relationship with your soul and to communicate with it regularly. It is recommended to tell your soul to always be with you and to be aware of yourself and your experiences in life.

It is necessary to consciously see events in your life as opportunities for growth and learning. It is important to be thankful for the problems and challenges that come your way, as they can offer valuable lessons and opportunities for personal growth.

Once you have learned and grown from a particular challenge, it is important to release it and ask for it to leave you. This helps to maintain a positive and healthy relationship with your soul and to continue on your path of personal growth and self-awareness.

Example - For the money Problem

Money problems have taught me the value of money and given my soul an important experience. I now understand the nature and worth of money problems. I ask that you leave me now. In the same way, it is important to approach any problem with a clear mind and to address it mentally.

Practice visualizing yourself being relieved of the problem every day. If you do this with sincerity and conviction, you will likely notice that the problem begins to disappear within one to three months.

It is important to approach this process with an open heart and soul, truly believing in the power of your thoughts and visualization to bring about positive change. Remember to keep a positive outlook and to approach every problem with determination and optimism.

This advice is based on my own personal experiences and the experiences of my friends. It is important to remember that everything that happens in life happens for a reason and for the greater good.

It is recommended to regularly communicate with your soul, encouraging it to grow and be positive, and reminding it that your body is its home. Ask your soul to protect itself from any negative energy and to only allow positive Reiki energy inside. This self-talk is known as a monologue.

With time and consistent practice, you may become aware of your soul responding to you, although this awareness may develop gradually rather than suddenly. Trust in the power of your thoughts and communication with your soul to bring about positive change and growth.

Symbol given at the last page

CHAPTER FIFTEEN

Reiki Symbol Energizing Technique

When we have free time, or when we are traveling and not occupied with other activities, it is easy to waste time. During these moments, it is a good idea to use the Reiki symbols to preserve and store your energy. You can take a mental note of the symbols and use them later during a healing session or when they are needed. This way, you can make the most of your free time and ensure that you always have a source of positive energy to draw upon.

Here is a step-by-step guide for energizing Reiki symbols:

- Start with a prayer to connect to the divine energy.
- Close your eyes and focus on the energy flowing into your hands.
- Visualize the 4th Reiki master symbol on the center of your palms.
- Imagine Reiki energy flowing from your hands into the symbol, filling it with energy and making it larger.
- Focus on this visualization for 1 to 2 minutes.
- Remove the symbol from your hands and store it in your mind.
- Repeat this process with the other Reiki symbols.

- Regularly energize the stored symbols whenever you have a spare moment to keep them active and ready for use.

Healing Process - After being energised

If the problem is your own, or if it is someone coming to you seeking healing, the person's/your plan is here, sickness or goal, whatever the sickness may be, these symbols can be used around it. Visualize any of the above

Step by Step Guide:

- Start with a prayer, connecting to the divine energy.
- Visualize one of the four symbols (4th, 1st, 2nd, 3rd) that you have already charged with energy.
- Imagine placing the symbols around the problem, illness, or goal of the person seeking healing or yourself.
- Place the 4th symbol above the 1st symbol on the left, the 2nd symbol below, and the 3rd symbol on the right.
- Mentally focus on the symbols and visualize Reiki energy flowing around the person or goal, improving its quality.
- Mentally communicate with the symbols, asking them to stay with the person or goal for as long as needed.
- Finally, imagine releasing the symbols into the sky and offer gratitude.

The Reiki symbols can be used at any time, whether it be during healing or while traveling. You can use this method for yourself or for others who are seeking healing. Daily practice of this technique will yield positive results. As you perform this healing, be sure to express gratitude to the Reiki energy and make a sincere wish for your goals or plans to come to fruition. It's important to remember that Reiki energy is a loving and divine energy, and it will only act in a way that aligns with what is truly best for you. If you have trouble visualizing the symbols, you can write them down on a piece of paper, hold it between your hands, and imagine Reiki energy enveloping it and soaring to the sky. When multiple individuals are seeking healing or when you have multiple desires, you can still use this method for each of them. The energized symbols in the sky will stay there until you thank the cosmic energy, so there's no need to repeatedly energize the symbols.

CHAPTER SIXTEEN

Shielding / Protection

Begin your practice with a prayer.

- Visualize yourself inside a large pyramid.
- Mentally speak to the pyramid, affirming its proper construction and design, and request that only divine energy is allowed within. Ask the pyramid to remove any negative or evil thoughts from yourself and ask for its protection. Imagine that you are surrounded by pure white light within the pyramid.
- You can also apply this technique for your loved ones, valuables, projects, or goals.
- Use the 4,1,2,3 symbols to visualize the ten sides of the pyramid. Repeat this visualization as many times as you like.

Securing goals through the pyramid

- Start with a prayer.
- Visualize yourself inside a large pyramid. Mentally affirm that the pyramid is constructed with the right measurements and only holds divine energy, and ask for any negative thoughts or energy to be removed from you.

- Imagine the person in need of healing or the goal you want to focus on is inside the pyramid with you.
- Mentally write the Reiki symbols 4,1,2,3 on the tip of the pyramid and call out the person's name or your goal's name three times while visualizing each symbol being written.
- Repeat the process of writing the symbols at the four corners of the pyramid, the four walls, and the earth. Use your two fingers or all fingers to write the symbols, not just one finger.
- Focus on feeling that the person's issue or your goal has been healed by the Reiki energy. Offer thanks to the Reiki Shakti and pray for your desired outcome. Stay in this visualization for as long as needed and feel a sense of protection for the person or goal.
- Finally, thank the Reiki Shakti and ask for your wishes to come true.

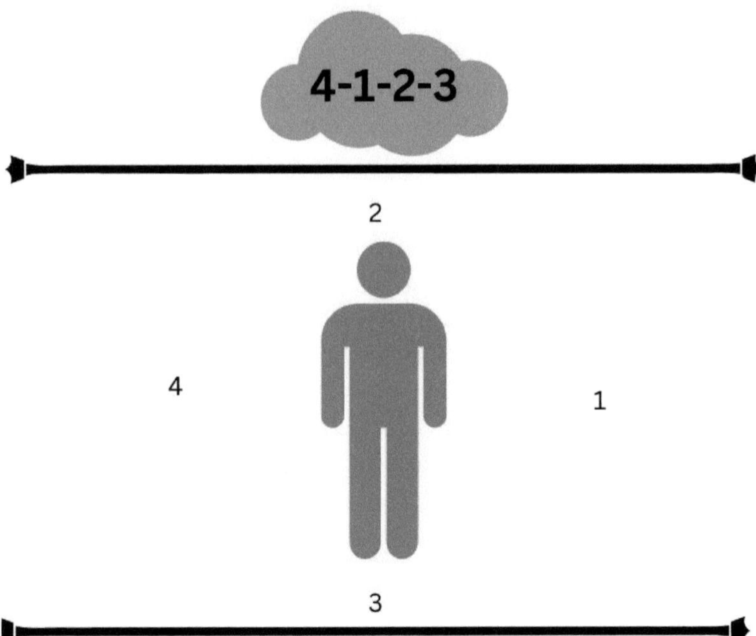

I performed exceptionally well in the interview on DD/MM/YYYY and I was successful in securing the job. I am grateful to Reiki Shakti and may your desires be accomplished.

CHAPTER SEVENTEEN

Psychic surgery

Psychic surgery is a special healing method that can cure physical, financial, emotional, and relationship problems, as well as remove negative energies, unwanted memories, curses, and bad feelings that block the flow of Reiki energy around a person or their chakras. This can be done through in-person healing or through distance healing techniques, and can be particularly effective for treating chronic or strange problems before other forms of healing.

Method of Psychic Surgery

- Begin by focusing on the problem, either by identifying its location or the amount of negative energy present.
- Stand in front of the subject and write the Reiki Master symbol (4th symbol) on your hand, repeating its name three times in your mind.
- Repeat the same process for symbols 1st, 2nd, and 3rd.
- Imagine your fingers extending with Reiki energy flowing from them, write symbol 1 on the negative energy and blow air from your mouth to direct the energy.
- Pray to your deity for effective healing.
- Mentally pull the negative energy into the Reiki energy and give it to your deity, repeating this process until improvement is noticed.

- Talk to the negative energy mentally, acknowledging that it has served its purpose and it is time for it to leave. Fill the space with positive Reiki energy and seal with the 1st symbol.
- Repeat the process on yourself for any negative energy you may have absorbed

CHAPTER EIGHTEEN

Reiki grid

This is similar to Sri Chakra which is a self-generating energy system that can be used for a variety of purposes, both big and small. By placing six pencil crystals along with a pyramid of crystals, a Reiki grid, also known as an antharkarna grid, can be created. The master crystal can be used to continuously flow cosmic energy for 48 hours by energizing it. This grid can be used to improve sleep by placing it under your pillow. It can also be used to energize medicines, fruits, and vegetables. There are two types of antharkarnas, male and female, and they can be used to achieve goals for both yourself and others.

Reiki Crystal Healing Grid requires 6 pencil crystals, 1 master crystal, 1 pyramid crystal, and 1 Antharkarna.

- Clean all crystals with salt water or running water.
- Place the crystals in a quiet and sacred space, where only you have access to it.
- Repeat the process of energizing the crystals 21 times, a total of 63 days.
- During this time, do not disturb or move the crystals until your goal has been achieved.

Image Courtesy - Pintrest

Reiki Crystal Charging Method

- Write your problem or place a photo in front of you.
- Perform the Energy Invoke and hold the Pyramid Crystal between your hands to give it energy.
- Place the Pyramid Crystal on top of the photo or project card.
- Hold the 6 pencil crystals between your palms, giving them Reiki energy, and arrange them in a circle around the Pyramid Crystal, with the tip of the pencils facing towards the Pyramid.
- Hold the Master Crystal between your palms and give it Reiki energy for 2-3 minutes, without touching the 6 pencil crystals.
- The Master Crystal will gently transfer the Reiki energy to the pencil crystals, starting with the first one.
- Give Reiki energy to the Pyramid Crystal by placing your hands slightly above it, without touching its tip.
- Give Reiki energy to the first pencil crystal for 2-3 minutes, and then continue to the second pencil crystal, repeating the process

until all 6 pencil crystals have been energized.

1st Pencil Crystal - Pyramid Crystal - 1st Pencil Crystal
(2min) - (2min) - (2min)
2nd Pencil Crystal - Pyramid Crystal – 2nd Pencil Crystal
(2min) - (2min) - (2min)
3rd Pencil Crystal - Pyramid Crystal – 3rd Pencil Crystal
(2min) - (2min) - (2min)

Write your problem or place a photo on the grid

- Invoke the energy and place the pyramid crystal between your hands, give it energy, and place it on the photo or problem card.
- Place the six pencil crystals between your palms, give them Reiki energy, and arrange them around the pyramid with the tip of the pencils pointing towards the pyramid.
- Place the master crystal between your palms and give it Reiki energy for 2-3 minutes, without touching any of the pencil crystals.
- Charge each of the pencil crystals with Reiki energy, starting with the first one. The master crystal should not touch any of the pencils or pyramids while charging, otherwise they will be disconnected from the energy. If it does touch, wash them in salt water or running water and start over.
- Remove the master crystal after charging, but keep in mind that this internal Reiki charge grid has the ability to flow continuously for 48 hours, but it's still recommended to energize the master crystal every 24 hours.
- Ensure that no crystal touches another crystal during the charging process.
- Optionally, you can meditate with the master crystal daily to keep it charged. If you're traveling, take your inner core photo and master crystal with you, and charge the inner core photo with your master crystal. This will keep the grid at home

charged as well.

Mode of writing requests (on slip / between hands) SMARTER Goal

- S - Specific
- M - Measurable
- A - Achievable
- R - Realistic
- T - Time bound
- E - Evaluation
- R - Reward

You can also fulfill all wishes by placing its cards together. Whatever desire you are healing, feel it happening.

Job interview

I performed exceptionally well in the interview on DD/MM/YYYY and I was successful in securing the job. I am grateful to Reiki Shakti and may your desires be accomplished.

To get back the lended amount

"With gratitude, I thank Reiki for helping me to retrieve my loan of Rs. [Amount]. The name of the lender was written on a slip and the loan was successfully returned to me. May Reiki's blessings be fulfilled."

Cheque method

Cheque inside the box of the pyramid and do as taught in the class.

To come out of bad habits

Thank you Reiki for guiding me towards this change and helping me to let go of this negative behavior. May your blessings continue to fill my mind with positivity and peace.

Cash flow

Thank you, Reiki, for your blessings and for making my financial life abundant and fulfilling. May your wish be fulfilled and may I continue to attract abundance and prosperity in all areas of my life.

While investing Money

I trust my financial instincts and make wise investments that bring me great returns. Money continues to flow into my life and I use it to create a secure and prosperous future. I am always grateful for the abundance and prosperity in my life. Thank you Reiki for guiding me towards financial stability and success.

To receive money

I attract abundance and prosperity in all aspects of my life, including money. I trust in the universe and its infinite resources, and I know that money is always flowing towards me. I am open and receptive to receiving this abundance, and I use it wisely to improve my life and the lives of those around me. I am grateful for the prosperity that is constantly coming into my life, and I am confident that my financial future is bright and abundant.

To Buy

I trust that my subconscious mind is guiding me to make the right choices and decisions when it comes to buying things. I am confident that it will bring me to the perfect item that I need and want, at the right price and in the right time. I am grateful for this inner guidance and trust in its wisdom.

Bride / groom selection

Visualize the qualities you desire in a partner, imagine the love and connection you both share, and let the universe do the rest. Remember to be patient, open-minded, and grateful, knowing that the right person will come into your life at the right time. I trust in the power of the universe and my subconscious mind to bring me the perfect partner, and I am grateful for this.

The conclusion

In conclusion, Reiki is a powerful form of energy healing that involves channeling universal energy to promote physical, emotional, and spiritual healing. There are four parts to Reiki, but it is only necessary to learn the first three parts. The fourth part is related to teacher training and is not mandatory, but it is recommended to learn the first three levels. Reiki works by creating a flow of energy around the body that can be captured by Kirlian photography, although it cannot be seen with the naked eye. By learning Reiki, one can harness the power of this energy to heal

CHAPTER NINETEEN

Steps for Conducting Counseling:

- Choose a calm and serene environment with soothing light and aromatic candles.
- Display relevant certificates and place a calendar for appointments.
- Use spiritual greetings to set the tone for the session.
- Arrange chairs in a comfortable and relaxed manner.
- Maintain your own dignity and dress appropriately in white, with a divine feel.
- Take a bath before the session using salt water to refresh and relax.
- Place a client registration form, water, tissues, a notebook, and a white hand towel on the table.
- Limit the counseling session to a maximum of one hour, with two appointments per person per week.
- Follow the 90/10 rule and listen actively to the client while maintaining a non-judgmental attitude.
- Place your phone on silent mode and ask the client to do the same.
- Allow the client to express their emotions, even if they start crying, as this can be a therapeutic release.
- Take regular breaks of 15-20 minutes for self-care during the session.

- Maintain a comfortable room temperature and keep devotional items in the room.
- Modulate your voice to match the client's and maintain eye contact to establish a connection.
- Give appropriate homework and keep in mind that you are a nurturing and caring figure for the client.
- Take a 30-minute break after lunch or eating before conducting the next session.

CHAPTER TWENTY

Progress Towards Life

- Acknowledge the reason for your problem: Take time to understand why your problem has arisen.
- Give gratitude: Express gratitude for the hardships, thanking them for the experiences they have given you in your life.
- Learn from the experience: Reflect on the lesson you have learned from your problems and how you can use it in the future.
- Pray for the problems to go away, but only if it is for the good of yourself and others.
- Reiki 4th Degree: Reiki 4th Degree, also known as Reiki Guru Deeksha, is an advanced level of Reiki training, but not mandatory.
- The symbols used in Reiki are sacred and secret, and should be ritually dissolved after use.
- Reiki vs medicine: Reiki is not a substitute for medicine, but it has been observed that using Reiki can reduce the need for medication.
- Role of a Reiki practitioner: Remember, as a Reiki practitioner, you are not a healer, but simply a conduit for the energy to flow through.
- Do not interfere with medical treatment and do not tell anyone to stop taking their medication.
- Leave it to the universe: After each healing, let Reiki know your wish for the best outcome, and leave it to the universe to take

care of the rest.

CHAPTER TWENTY-ONE

Life meditation

- Avoid using swear words as they can harm you. Trust that others will believe in your honesty without the need for proof through swearing.
- Show gratitude towards those who assist you. Stand in front of a mirror, acknowledge your mistakes with your hands over your heart, forgive yourself and others for their mistakes, and do not allow negative thoughts to control your mind.
- Give 10% of your earnings to those in need without publicizing it. The Law of Karma dictates that you will receive 10 times what you give. Plant positive seeds for a positive outcome.
- Speak with your soul, maintain a pure state and prevent negative energies from entering. List and solve your problems one by one.
- Wear armor and sprinkle salt in the corners of your home as a form of protection. While mopping, add salt to the water for added protection.
- Focus on your goals but don't be consumed by petty desires. Practice Super Brine Yoga and daily white light meditation. Use the Rubber Band Technique and Nidhidhysa meditation when faced with challenges.
- Live in the present moment and find happiness in what you have instead of constantly focusing on what you lack. Astrology can be believed in, but it's not necessary for living.
- Express gratitude for what you have, including basic comforts. Offer thanks to God at least twice a week.

- Avoid unnecessary borrowing and pay off any credit card debt. Live a simple and humble life and avoid comparing yourself to others.
- See difficulties in your life as opportunities for growth and record the lessons learned in a diary. Reflect on these lessons regularly to see personal improvement over time.
-

Savikalpa Holistic Center Mysore

Mobile 6364795551/9538735551
Youtube- @ Savikalpaholisticcenter
Facebook Savikalpaholisticcenter

Secret Symbols Cho-ku-rei

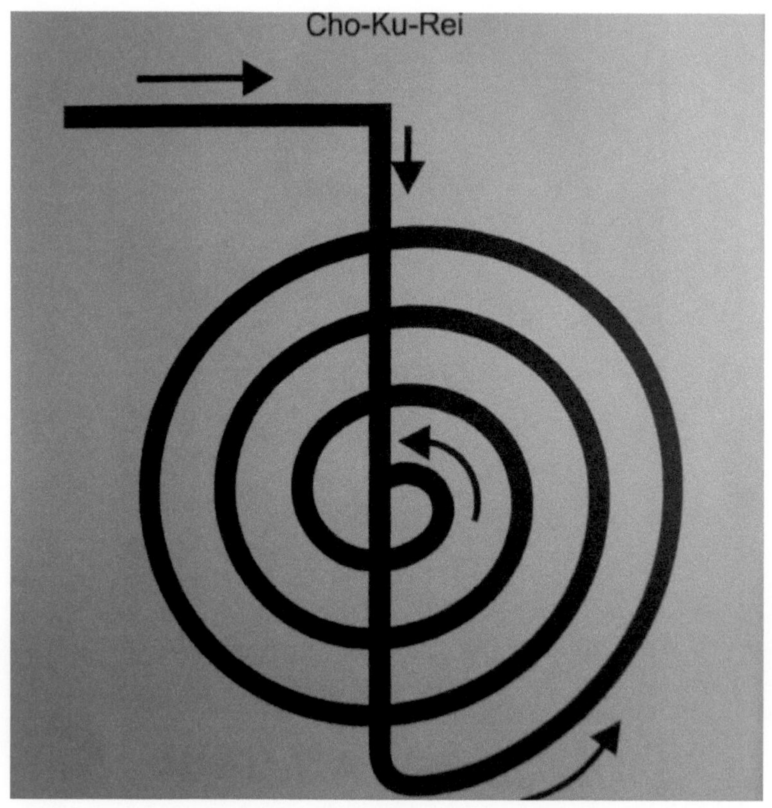

Savikalpa Holistic Center Mysore

Mobile 6364795551/9538735551
Youtube- @ Savikalpaholisticcenter
Facebook Savikalpaholisticcenter

Secret Symbol - Se-he-kie

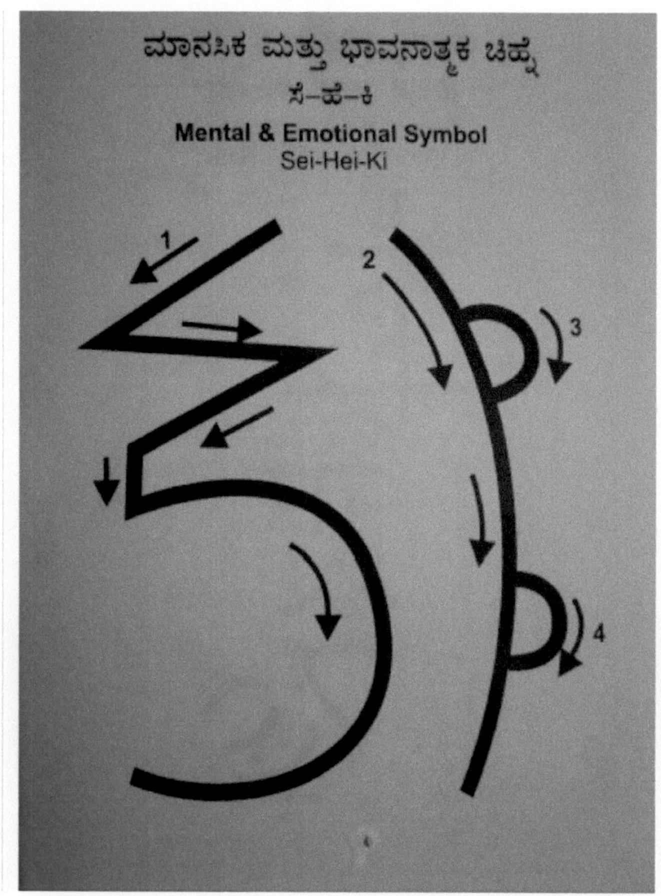

Savikalpa Holistic Center Mysore

Mobile 6364795551/9538735551

Youtube- @ Savikalpaholisticcenter

Facebook Savikalpaholisticcenter

Secret Symbol- Han-sha-jesho-nen

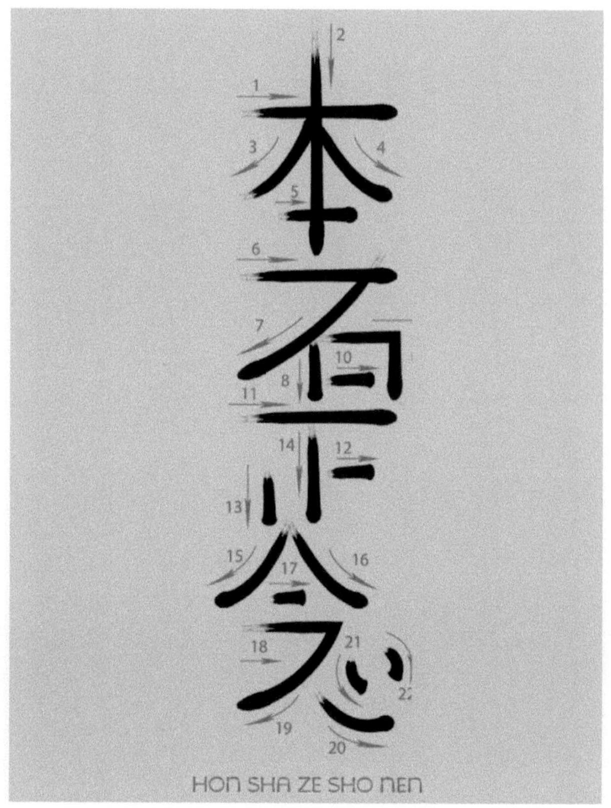

Savikalpa Holistic Center Mysore

Mobile 6364795551/9538735551

Youtube- @ Savikalpaholisticcenter

Facebook Savikalpaholisticcenter

Secret Symbol- Dy-ko-myo

Dai Ko Myo

Our Media Coverage

Class Memories

Enter Caption

df

Enter Caption

Notes

Notes

Notes

Notes

Notes

Notes

Free 1-2-1 Session

Since you bought this book you will have free 1-2-1 session for 30 mins with us. (depends available of the slot)

Savikalpa Holistic Center Mysore

Mobile 6364795551/9538735551
Youtube- @ Savikalpaholisticcenter
Facebook Savikalpaholisticcenter

9 798889 754145